WELCOME TO

DEAF POETRY SLAM

TABLE OF CONTENTS

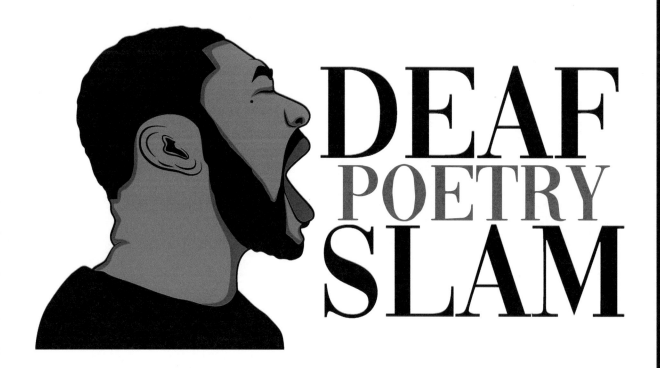

Printed in the United States of America

First Printing, 2024

ISBN 9798877977464

Out The Water Productions
911 Robinwood Ave Suite B
Whitehall, OH 43213

www.DeafPoetrySlam.com

DEDICATION
DEAF POETRY SLAM

A journey can often take a lifetime to reach the destination that one sees in their vision.

However, the fulfillment is in the process as it provides us the substance we need to overcome and achieve the obstacles that life brings.

The completion of Deaf Poetry Slam has been that journey for me. Having the opportunity to work through the struggle of developing a piece of art work that I can dedicate to the people!

My life experiences I get to share with the world in hopes that these words will wake up the slumber thoughts and ideas and mostly the actions of the individual who seeks to go and be great…!

Dad, you are missed beyond any words i can share on paper or in a speech. Your wisdom remains with me daily as i continue the journey. I am grateful for the years i was able to share with you. As we are only promised a ripple in this ocean, know that your ripple made a major impact and contribution to the wave of life!

I Love You

Mom, your unwavering love is exactly what God intended for a mother to give to her son. Know i overflow with love because you decided to love me so much. God is pleased.

I Love You

ACKNOWLEDGMENTS
DEAF POETRY SLAM

To my design artist Mariah Carlos you have been a God Send and perfect timing for us to meet and work together on this project. This is an example of patience and allowing The Most High to truly connect to the right people at the right times. Thank you and I look forward to us doing more amazing work to share with the world!

To The Wife… Thank you for allowing me the space and time to achieve one of my life's works as you dedicated yourself to the daily activities of the family ensuring that a beat in the song is not missed during the production…! My Heart

To My Children … you have something to share with yourself and with your children that can be passed down and appreciated and used as motivation to overcome and accomplish anything you put your heart and mind and action into…! It is because of you that I know the greatest things are still yet to come.

The Most High, Thank you for the gifts you have bestowed upon me. It's a pleasure to receive yet most of all be in action with the will and talents. You trusted me with this vision and I trust in you to continue to move this vision forward!

Ase' and Amen

ABOUT THE AUTHOR
DEAF POETRY SLAM

Markus has lived a life considered as the best and worse of both worlds encountering several situations and circumstances of challenge and change.

These encounters have helped him experience intercontinental travel as well as international travel. These travel adventures have energized, educate, and shape the mind expressed with us in this timeless art.

His many perspectives on life have created ingredients to turn his interactions into his artistic interpretations.

He carries wisdom from varying encounters in education, street life, mentor, as a father, a husband, a friend, a brother, and a son. He has collaborated those perspectives into a diverse collection of those mindsets and developed words of art for all to enjoy.

Welcome To Deaf Poetry Slam!

JUST
POETRY

I dare you to seek gratification

I dare you to have patience

Become a part of the manifestation

And do away with all the simple hating

It's for righteousness I have a serious craving.

Is it enough to just love and give big hugs? Or am I wrong because in the back of my mind I hope to meet the plug?

We all are accustomed to our own drugs.

Sometimes I question if God is love. But who the hell am I so you be the judge. I'm optimistic, try not to hold a grudge.

I'm over it. So why she scolding it? I feel my heart and there's cold in it. I'm trying to remove the fear and put bold in it.

I've got power. Is it because of the gun I'm holding? Maybe it's the car I'm rolling! Is it the bank account with legal money I've stolen?

These aren't just words, it's poetry designed to fill the mind, body, and souls of you and me!

I GOT
DREAMS

I'm lying here dreaming, got these visions in my mind... Seed has been planted, I'm trying to get this water so I can take advantage of the fruits from this labor...

Because I got dreams that are greater... What's stopping me is this hater, within me is the savior...

With him I gain favor, and it's not because he liked my flavor. He is no respecter of person, regardless whoever sets foot on this earth

I'm graced with His birth, death, and resurrec- tion. Faced with His hurt as the disciples left in the opposite direction

Feared the unknown until I realized that He is the throne. I got dreams that I am realizing, I can't manifest on my own.

I need a team, but understand we can't look back as we must know we will be turned to stone. God looked at me and said, "What should I do with these dry bones?"

I said, "I got dreams allow me to proceed be- fore you decide it's time to call me home."

So here I am in my youth though I look grown. He said, "You can't enter the kingdom of heaven unless your like a child with a soft tone."

hhHumbled, I got dreams!

MY
HEART

My heart is filled with love, touched by your every word. I'm delighed in your view.

They say absence makes the heart yearn more for you! If I didn't believe before I'm sure now it's truth.

Evidence is in the present events. Trapped by my heart as I do my best to represent.

You are my heart and no I don't know how or why. So I'm going to just enjoy this even if it's only for a short period of time...!

I'M
LEARNING

I'm learning to separate my disgust in this world from my grind.
delighed in your view.
I'm learning that the only way there can be no child left behind...

Is if I act more than I complain... Is if I stack more so I can gain... Is If I
impact more than I drain. If I put on more smiles, rather induce pain.

I'm learning that the only chains are those wrapped around my
brain...

Caused by a social society that's too busy denying me... Too
busy deifying me... Too busy lying to me... Doing its best to keep
trying me by keeping me behind the scenes.

I'm learning that a voice can be heard...

If you gather up the courage to share a few words. If you open up
your wings and fly like a bird.

If we make the choice to allow God to purge the spirit, mind, body,
& soul. I'm learning that I gotta love truth more than I do...silver &
gold!!!

THE
FACT IS

The fact is we live in a society where we are attracted to false advertising, fake analyzing, and what always seems to be wrong timing.

The fact is everyone is concerned with everyone else's tactics. Resulting in many of us doing things backwards, similar to Hollywood and its actors.

The fact is racism is still replaced with subliminal hate, regenerating slavery continuously even until today.

The fact is we continue to clash here because fate, destiny, and the hand has already delivered what it practiced. The past is the present and the future. The problem is rather or not we abide by the teacher.

The fact is inside of me is everything I'm lacking. However, I got this picture put up by the media that tells me what's attractive.

The fact is they give us reality TV to show us how we're acting. Too bad we can't realize that there has been a hijacking. A mental falsehood and all it does is subtract them.

The fact is I'm labeled by a people who builds stories that are fables. Like a horse trapped in its stable ready to run this race I'm a stallion

The fact is... What is it that you will teach threw your practice...?

CONFRONT
IT

It's sad that we are ok with concepts like its momma's baby, daddy's maybe.

Or she won't let me see my baby because she hates me. When in reality part of the reason is simply amazing because as a father nothing can separate me from my baby.

Nope, not bars in the hood or bars from a cell, financially I'm there even when I'm not doing well. I'm in the court room giving them hell. See when it comes to my seed I'm a represent them well.

Today we are seeing lazy and passive people giving in to a necessary evil. Confront it.

Head on I am with the collision understanding as a young man God has given me vision. Though my path may be a little different I'm still faced with the same mission.

Out here it is considered survival of the fittest. Or crabs in a basket fighting for a position.

With so many in your ear trying to get you to keep tradition. Not realizing that's what got people out here now signing petitions.

The truth hurts. Confront it. It's my job to give it to you regardless if you want it. Confront it.

It's my duty to keep it 100.

WHAT DOES IT MEAN
TO BE LOVED?

Passion with a side of character. This love thing seems to have a lot of arrogance.

I thought love was a one way street. I run into you, you run into me.

Then it becomes we, but it seems that we just aren't in too deep.

Consciously, I'm thinking about her and your thinking about he.

The problem is neither of them are you or me. I try to be spontaneous with a combustion.

But it seems like my thoughts are wrong just like my touches.

What does it mean to be loved in, on?

It said if two come together let them join in, on...

I guess this is just the same old song!

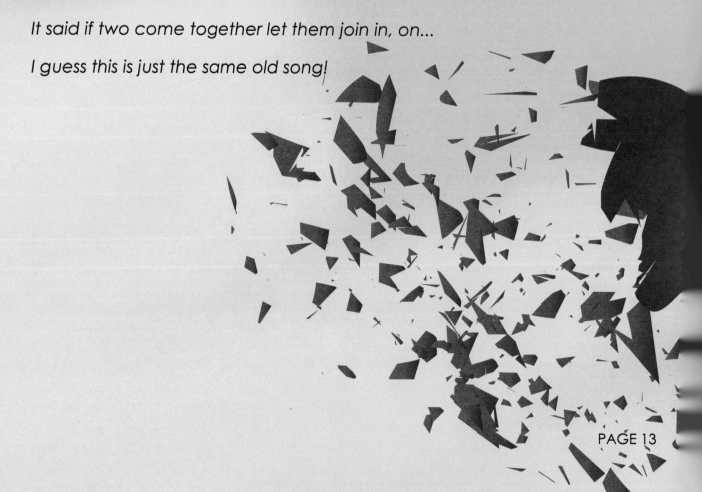

LOVE IS

Love is a basic emotion ready to share. But the problem is most of us are scared. Afraid to let go... Afraid to give in... Afraid that love has no end.

So I put this ink down to share love with a friend... Dear to my heart even after this ends. Life as we know it only to meet again.

Hoping we remember that it was love we were after. Love that first started this chapter. Love that kept us during the pressure as it amounted to more than what we thought we could bear.

Love is a magnet ready to attract it... More of it... In store of it is your soul... Spirit... And heart. God has kept us with not just His grace... But more because Love is...

Love is... the wind beneath the wings... the fantasy and the dream. Love is... character, personality without the barriers.

WHERE DO WE GO
FROM HERE?

I was presented with this question from a family member, a friend, one who I admire in spite of their current situation and circumstance because I know that they have asked themselves the question, where do we go from here? So...

Where do we go from here? A place of silence and despair where only sighs and tears remain fair.

Where do we go from here? A mindset that is tainted by the ways of life... The facts of life... Through the trials and tribulations of all that is trifle...

Where do we go from here? Sadden by the moments of sudden loss but forced to mature and be responsible for the cost even though I didn't put in the application with the boss.

Where do we go from here? Filled with the guidance of life often called soul and spirit but it seems right now I can't see, smell, or hear it. Before now I didn't know what fear is.

Where do we go from here? Built up anger because those I loved have been replaced with strangers.

Where do I go from here? Get polished... Buffed out by the best detailer known to man. So I ask...

Where do we go from here? It is my hope to be healed... Only to be filled with weapons of positive deposits such as wisdom and knowledge which both can be begotten without attending college. Or staying in the hood wheremy prosperity is being held hostage.

PERSONAL
GAIN

It's all for personal gain... Is it fame, fortune, or those things that leave a stain on the heart?

Art is an expression of our soul's **in-depth-ness** *how our spirit and soul is young and restless, doing its best to stay connected to the one who described us best!*

It's all for personal gain...

So I blame you, you, and you. The leader of the Klu, Klux, Klan, the NAACP too, and those who claim to be **TRU... Without the E...**

I guess I should stay on surface because I will lose you all if I take it too deep. Like 6 feet below and or beneath all that matters.

Your matter is no longer of matter because you no longer exist regardless if you are here with intent and purpose if you are not acting on it or in it...! Who or what is it and you?

It's all for personal gain... I change as I am be- coming... All that is and was I am that which is and was because I am here for what's in it for me even when I give because when I come I come in peace. It is He that dwells in me... If not, it would all be for personal gain...!

It's all for personal gain...

DESPERATE
MEASURES

Can the sun shine in the darkest of hours? Provide light in the darkness of ours.

Heart to Heart seems to be farther from love. Bearing down Lord we need your hand and hugs.

Scattered across these great nations. Desperate measures so many are taking.

Raging evil rampantly racing to steal the joy of those patiently waiting... to grow.

So I am grieved for the world and I want it to know that desperate measures no longer will hold...

Each of us hostage...in a world where freedom is bondage.

In a world where we should be focused on what we have in common.

Let me take a second to pay homage to those who are caught in the cross fire of our dominance.

Those who have fallen victim to greed for the benefit of our prominence Lord you are the author of all things good. So I pray you restore as only you could

Desperate Measures.

IT'S MEAN
OUT HERE!

*It's mean out here, everybody out for green out here. We're such individuals we can't even form a
team out here.*

I wish everybody was color blind like the movie "Pleasantville"

Before they discovered what it meant to have what we call a good time.

Sex, drugs, and money became the new state of mind.

*Music took over, nobody's sober. It's like being at the concert calling this dude name J, HOVA. Now
don't look over, and don't overlook. But those who may seem unrighteous really are the crooks.*

Double take, I took a second look.

Be cautious Lil fishes, these fisherman are vi- cious...eager to get you on the hook.

*Keeping us shook with situations and circum- stances like 9-11, Aurora, and Sandy Hook.
Entertained by movies, music, and shows like "The Game" only to have your mind, body, and spirit
"Detained" for entry.*

*My bad don't mind me, I'm just speaking on the things we enjoy daily.The things that con- tinue to
fade me or should I say faze me...out.*

STAND UP

This is a place of refugee a place to be you.

This is a place of protection...where we speak and receive truth.

This is a place of destiny built by Gods hands...

This is a place where we celebrate Pastor Sue Caesar Alexander and...

This is a place excited to provide a second chance...

This is a place where Christ is your number one fan.

This is a place where I feel as if everyone is FAM.

So I Say...

Stand up, put your hands up your under arrest for the crime of the lack of time that you have invested in yourself

And all I hear you saying is you wanna have... What? And all I hear you saying is you wanna get...What?

Chances are you're going to get stuck in be- tween a rock and a hard place...a small space, having to realize that this is all faith...

And if you don't believe then possible this is all fate. Then understand that your life is in a RAW state.

Able to be placed in danger... But if it was truly up to you... Wouldn't you want to be in good hands like **ALL STATE?**

Have you been gone for so long...? Have you been so right that you can't see your wrong?

So I Say...

Stand up, put your hands up your under arrest for the crime of the lack of time that you have invested in yourself.

CRASH

Reckless endangerment, a change in lanes... Don't crash the vehicle while changing lanes...

Is this the vehicle that can change the game? Or is this the car that caused all the pain?

The car that put you on the road to fame? After the accident we are always looking for others to blame...

It's hard work with much more to gain...but to keep doing it over and expecting a different results insane...

A crash victim...the blast hit them...fortunate death skipped them. Here is another chance. Not everybody gets the chance to advance...

Potentially could be that last daddy daughter dance. Damn, it feels like I've driven the car off a dam...

If only I would have stuck to the plans... I wouldn't be the victim in this crash again, and again, and again!

WHAT IS JUSTICE?

What is justice? Is it for just us? Meaning a Human being looking for a super being.

Is there truth in this term? Is there definition in the meaning? What's the identity of justice? Is it the choice to be feed up and confess up?

Is it the death of us? Or the birth of trust? What is justice? Has the time and situation confused us? Do you choose or does justice choose us?

The argument is what's the fuss? It has been served, you heard the words now is the time to gird... Up your loins. There is a time for every- thing including to mourn. A time to be reborn, a time when justice can have us all torn.

Does justice allow you to wear your horns? Does justice remind you of those thorns in your side? Those thorns that help you decide... justice. Is it for just us?

I hope as I pray that today is the day that we begin to learn that what we are can never compare to who we are.

By far created greater than you have ever stated. Never could have made it if I knew for you... What is justice? Is it just us?

DEAF POETRY SLAM

When I slam these words that you can't hear... I recognize that you have what many call deaf ears...

Deaf from all the things that may be caused by fear... fear of things that once drawled tears...

Peace be still as my poetry slams each of you that choose to stay deaf...Today I must play the role of not judge, jury, but ref.

If you didn't allow it to fall on deaf ears... slammed it when it needed to be lifted up... that was the moment to gain a little bit of its trust.

Deaf and possibly muted from all the mockery... The pressure of someone telling me what's good and what's not for me... Only to find out that they have words that are delivered with hypocrisy...

My words are for those who practice mass agony... Those words that slam the ears with a frequency of poetry. Designed to hopefully enlighten him, her, them, and me.

So when I'm given the opportunity to speak I hope my **Deaf Poetry Slam** is everything we need...!

PRIDE IS AMAZING

Pride is amazing isn't it? It's amazing how it can keep you from the things you are compelled to do.

It is amazing how it keeps you bottled up. Wrapped up in independence not even considering if you can win or lose.

It is believed we are a being that has the ability to be limitless created by a God who has creativity that is endless.

So how do you suppose that the prideful ego would attempt to end this? By death through temptation and destruction. See it's at this point when many of us started cussing. Or doing a whole lot of fussing but in reality talking and doing nothing.

Or in other words doing the opposite of creating and that is the whole meaning when it speaks on pride being a cause of destruction. Or the reason why these young black boys keep busting, and busting, and busting. It's almost oxymoron because they busting guns at their sons while busting nuts in his mother.

Pride is amazing isn't it? It's too bad these words hit the mind and curve past your sense of direction.

It's pride that smiles on the outside. While inside there's heckling. Dr. Jackal and Mr. Hyde.

Pride is Amazing isn't it?

CLOSING REMARKS

Deaf Poetry Slam wants to thank all supporters who have come out to events, purchased books and merch. Your love and support is everything!

It is my hope that this information, these words have reigned down on each of you and your families and provided you with insight, inspiration, motivation, and faith to continue on through every concern, every issue that takes time out of our day to implement a negative impact.

Deaf Poetry Slam seeks to bless the people through words of wisdom, positive energy that resonates with the grace and peace of God.

Thank you for your Love...! Grace and Peace be with you!

Markus A. Johns (M. A. Johns) AKA H. I. M. (Highest In Me)

DEAF POETRY SLAM
(POETRY IN MOTION)

THANK YOU

LET'S GET SOCIAL!

FACEBOOK
DeafPoetrySlam

INSTAGRAM
DeafPoetrySlam

EMAIL
DeafPoetrySlam@Gmail.com

X
DeafPoetrySlam

WEBSITE
www.DeafPoetrySlam.com

Made in the USA
Columbia, SC
29 July 2024

39456469R00024